Chain﹖ ﹖ ﹖ Bowl

A Complete Step-By-Step Guide

John K. Woodmann

Introduction

Create a unique wooden bowl with the help of these step-by-step guide.

The following instructions will help you to reduce mistakes in the production.

You can produce a bowl with chainsaw, chisel, mallet, steel brush and sandpaper in 5 hours.

Table of Contents

Basics

The truth about carving is:

- Start! A long way begins with one single step.

- Begin with an easy project!

- With the help of patterns you can produce your first sculpture easier. Draw the sculpture on paper. Make a model out of clay.

Tools

You need almost obligatorily a chainsaw to produce the rough form and to hollow out the bowl. You can do that also without chainsaw, however this increases the time you need immensely.

You can clamp the steel brushes in an angle grinder or a drill. Should you want to produce several bowls, you may think about the acquisition of a small angle grinder. The drills are not made for the long use of steel brushes.

A smoothing plane removes the remaining not-needed wood very fast. With some patience you can rub away the superfluous wood. Electric sanding machines make the work way easier.

You will find out further details about the application of the single tools in the following chapters.

Work Safety

Do not attempt to operate the tools without proper safety equipment and thorough knowledge of the operation, as based on the manufacturer's guidelines!

During the work with a chainsaw it is also recommended to wear cut protection trousers, industrial safety shoes, a helmet with visor and ear protection.

When working with an electric steel brush it is important to wear protection goggles.

Fine wooden dust (e.g., from the oak) is in the suspicion of being cancer-causing. Use a respirator during the grinding work.

Raw Material

In principle you can use every type of wood for the production of a sculpture.

Texture:
The stronger a texture is recognizable, the more interesting becomes the sculpture. Root wood is very individual.

Species of wood:
Use wood which can be carved well. Good to use are many broad-leaved trees, for example: lime-tree, chestnut, birch or pear.

Drying:
The wood does not necessarily have to be dry. You can produce the sculpture also of undried wood if the sculpture requires no dimensional accuracy. Certain species of wood (e.g., beech) tear very strongly when being dried. These species of wood should, if possible not be used undried. Sculptures of undried wood should not be thick - otherwise the possibility that you will tear is very high.

Sawing Raw Material

Give the desired raw form to the basic material. Use a saw. I always use a chainsaw.

Carving Bowls

For the production of wooden bowls you should try to take wood with special structure (branches, roots...). Use irregularities. You give a special individual mark to the sculpture. The bowl thereby becomes a unique specimen, special in the era of machine-made goods.

The following described production steps are only one suggestion.

Shaping the Outside of the Bowl

Try to shape the outside in the final form. I use an electric smoothing plane and an electric sander. Shape in direction of fibre to avoid splitting off wood.

Give the bowl ground an arched form. Remove a little bit more wood in the middle than on the left and on the right. Thereby the bowl does not wobble later on.

Hollowing of the Bowl

Hollowing the bowl can simply be done with chainsaw and chisel. Saw about 3 cm deep cuts in the inside (in the corner of 90 ° to each other).

Fix the wooden bowl in such a way that you have both of your hands for working with the chainsaw. The fixation is possible between 3 bigger chunks of wood (on the left, on the right and behind - see the following picture).

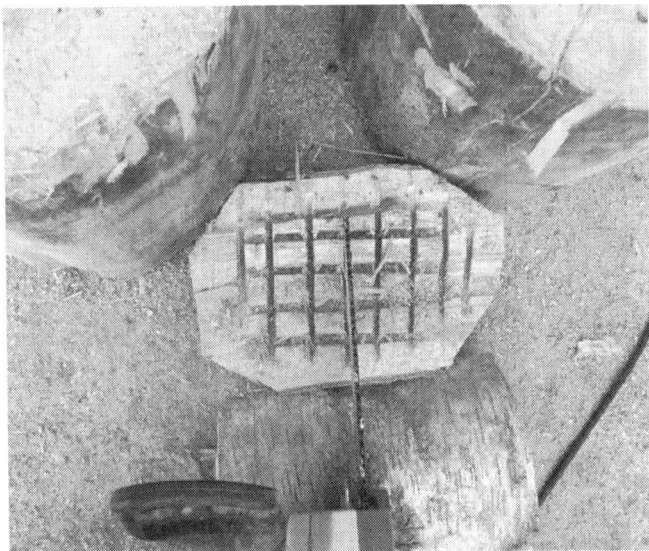

Remove the resulted blocks with the chisel and a
wooden mallet.

Repeat this, until you have reached 2/3 of the desired
depth.

Sawing inside the Bowl

Remove the last third with a chainsaw. The thickness of the wall of your bowl after this should at least be 1 cm. You need no special carver bar for these tasks. You can perform this step without chainsaw oil. In this case the bowl is not soiled with chainsaw oil. However, this leads to increased abrasion of all not oiled parts of the chainsaw (chain, sword).

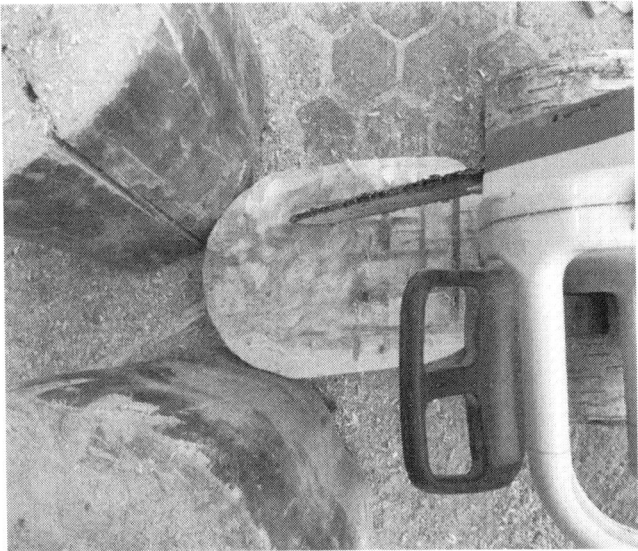

Shaping the Bowl with a Steel Brush

A twisted steel brush (see picture below on the right) removed superfluous wood very well. There are very different steel brushes, with very different properties. The shorter the wires (see picture below middle), the greater the effect. Untwisted wires (see picture below on the left) have a lower effect than twisted wires (see picture below on the right).

Use an angle grinder or a drill.

If the wood becomes black you should remove the black spots with the sanding machine.

Sanding the Bowl

Grind the outside of the bowl. Check whether the bowl stands properly on a straight tabletop.

You can grind the inside of the bowl with an pad sander or manually.

Brushing the Surface

Brush the surface with a long untwisted steel brush with low speed. In this way the bowl receives a rustic appearance. Pay attention to the direction of the wooden grain. Never change the rotation direction. You avoid a strong wear of the steel brush. The wires break off very fast by change of the rotation direction.

Renounce brushing the surface, if you desire a
smooth surface.

Branding the Logo

Brand a logo in the bowl with the soldering iron.
Afterwards slur the logo with sandpaper.

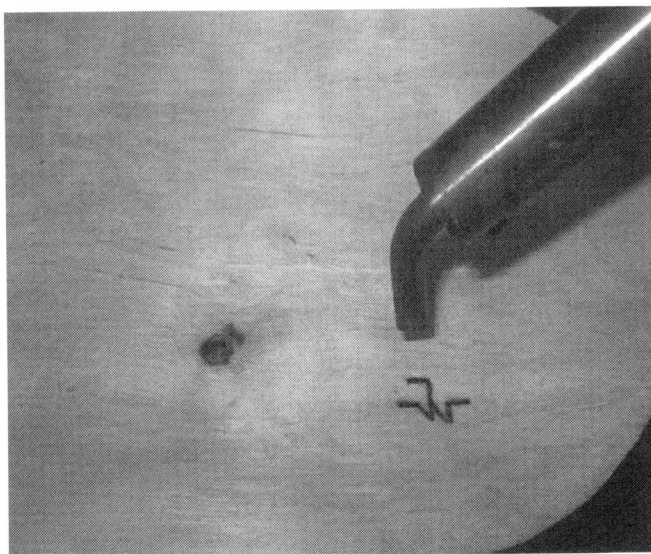

Varnishing

Varnish the bowl with colourless parquet varnish
(high durability). After the first varnish painting you
must sand again from hand. Afterwards you must
varnish again and sand afterwards again. You can dry
the bowl on big screws with strong thread. Thereby
you avoid imprints almost completely.

Before varnishing you can stain the wood with
another colour. Then you must stain, varnish, sand,
stain, varnish, sand.

Decoration Proposals

If you give away the bowl as an present, decorate the bowl with flowers or fruit. No limits are set to your imagination.

Maintaining the Tools

You can work much better with sharp tools.

Sharpening the Chainsaw

You can sharpen the chain of the chainsaw simply yourself. Buy a chainsaw sharpness set consisting of a round file, flat file and filing gauge.

Please note that the diameter of the round file is suitable for the chain. If you are not sure, consult a specialist.

You can find very good instructions under: http://www.stihl.com/saegeketten-schaerfen.aspx

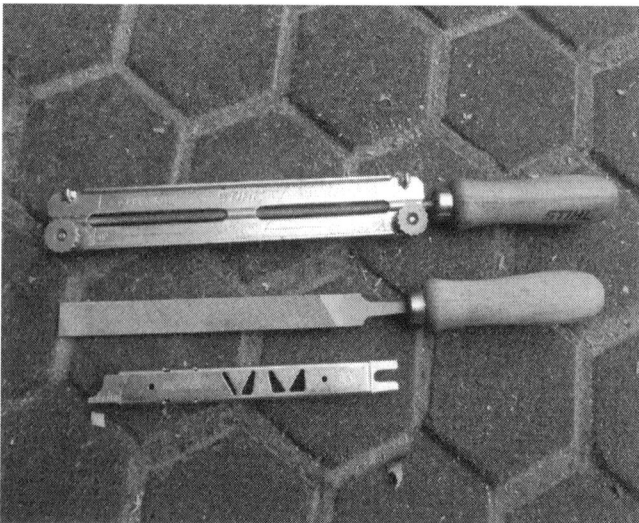

Fix the carver bar of the chainsaw in a clamping device. Arrest the chain with the chain brake.

Hold the file like given on the filing gauge. Normally 3 file movements per incisor should be sufficient. In this case less is more.

Sharpen so all incisors.

The minimum size of the tooth is marked on the incisors. If the minimum size is reached you must exchange the chain for a new chain.

By the purchase please remember that, all parameters of the old chain (length, number of chain links, form of the chain links) must correspond to the new chain.

Control the depth limiter (see picture below). The
depth limiter must be smaller than the sawtooth.

If necessary you must file something off the depth limiter.

Sharpening the Chisel

You can sharpen the chisels, knives... simply yourself.

Hold the chisel as shown in the following picture.

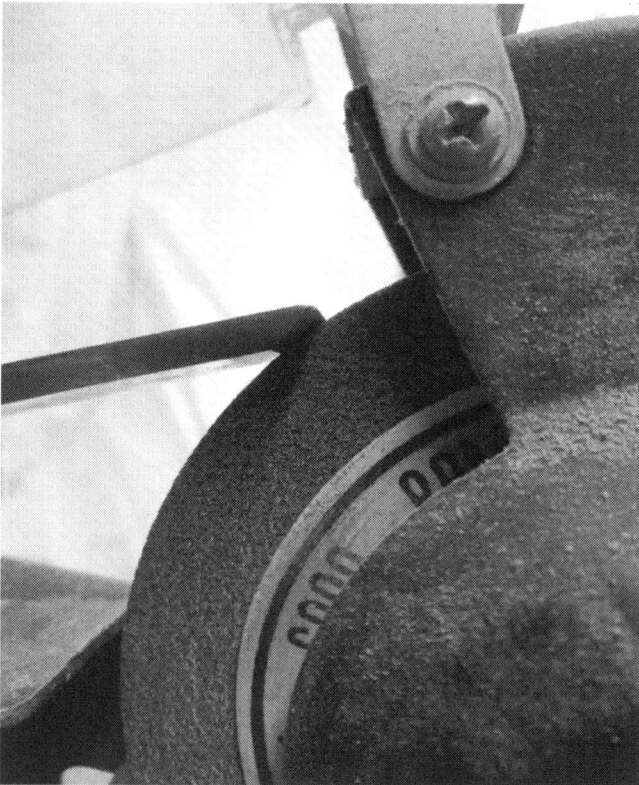

Cool the tools regularly with water.

You can find very good instructions under:
http://woodturninglearn.net/articles/sharpen1.htm

9574707R00020

Printed in Great Britain
by Amazon.co.uk, Ltd.,
Marston Gate.